Robert Nye is a distinguished writer of poetry, drama and fiction for adults and children, and is a regular reviewer of fiction. His adult novels include *Falstaff*, *Merlin*, *Faust* and *Mrs Shakespeare*. This brilliant retelling of *Beowulf* has sold over a quarter of a million copies in America. Robert Nye lives in County Cork in the Republic of Ireland.

D0318797

BEOWULF

ROBERT NYE

Orion
Children's Books

First published in Great Britain
by Faber and Faber in 1968
Originally published in the USA
by Hill and Wang in 1968

First published in paperback in 1995
This edition published in 2004
by Dolphin paperbacks
an imprint of the Orion Publishing Group Ltd
Orion House
5 Upper St Martin's Lane
London WC2H 9EA
An Hachette Livre UK Company
Hardback edition published in 1994
by Orion Children's Books

7 9 10 8

A catalogue record for this book
is available from the British Library.

Printed in Great Britain by
Clays Ltd, St Ives plc

ISBN 978 1 85881 076 8

www.orionbooks.co.uk

For my son Jack

Contents

1
A SHIP
WITHOUT
A SAIL

L ong ago there was no King in the land of the Danes, and they all wanted one. When a ship without sails or sailors came drifting in from sea, they went to meet it looking for a wonder, and sure enough there was a child in the ship. The child was curled asleep on a sheaf of ripe corn, with gold and swords heaped round about him. A golden flag flapped at the mast.

'This is Odin's doing!' cried a fisherman with a big white beard that blew in the wind like spindrift. 'We need a king, and he sends us this child across the sea. I'm sure he is a prince.'

'Of course he is,' said someone else. 'Look at his clenched fists and the way he smiles in his dreams. Oh, he's royal all right!'

'Perhaps he is Odin's son,' said a third.

Now, Odin was a great god. So the child was taken gently from the ship and wrapped in rich robes and hailed as ruler of all the Danes. They called him Scyld Scefing.

Scyld grew up to be strong and brave, the terror of his enemies. He was tall as a tower and his eyes blazed like bonfires when he was angry. Running into battle, he could shout so loud that men felt the cry like a hammer on their heads, and fell down dead of fright. His sword was so long and heavy that no one else could lift it. His horned helmet was big enough to put an eagle in. When he sat down to supper, in a chair carved out of a whole oak tree, the cooks ran to and fro bringing him bulls to eat, and barrels of beer that he drained in one go. His laughter cracked stones.

For all this, Scyld Scefing was kind and wise, and his people loved him. Under his rule, peace came to the land of the Danes, because none of the neighbour countries dared to fight with such a giant. Instead, they brought him gifts and tributes so that he would not go to war against them. The treasury swelled until it was like a hill of jewels.

At last Scyld grew to be an old man. His stride was still enormous, but no longer did his feet strike thunder from the earth. His body bent and his eyes – which once could have outstared the sun – grew watery. He could not eat a whole bull any more.

Scyld knew his end was near. He called his warriors to him and told them what they must do.

'Build me a great ship,' he said, his trumpet tongue now shrunken to a whisper, 'and let the decks of the ship be strewn with gold, and swords stacked upon the gold. And hang my shield and corselet in the prow, that the waves may know me and show respect. And in the heart of the ship, under the tall mast that must have no sail, prepare a bed that will burn. And in the heart of the bed let a sheaf of corn be planted.'

His warriors were sad, but they did as he said. Scyld lay on a silver litter at the water's edge and watched with tears as the ship was made ready. When all had been done as he had commanded, he dragged himself on board and lay down on the bed. They piled jewels on his chest where the great heart beat uncertainly, like the footfalls of a messenger near journey's end. They saluted him, one after another, and returned to the shore in silence. Dawn was coming, and the air smelt salty cold.

The sheaf of corn flickered into thin green flame. Then it was gold and raging. The whole ship blazed as it moved against the wind and out to the waiting sea.

2
A HALL
FULL OF
BLOOD

Scyld Scefing left a son who ruled after him, and that son had another son, named Healfdene. Healfdene had three sons, Hrothgar, Heorogar, and Halga, and a daughter whose name has been forgotten, although she was beautiful and witty and married Onela, king of the Swedes. All Scyld's heirs had some of Scyld in them, though none had quite such giant strength. Of the three sons of Healfdene, Hrothgar was strongest, and when his father died they made him king.

Hrothgar had a backbone that would bend to no man. He was bold and fierce, with red hair, a jutting jaw, and eyes like naked swords. While still a boy, he had killed a bear with his own hands. It was not a particularly big bear, but the deed was sufficient to make him famous. Hrothgar himself did not boast, but his poets sang his praises all over the land of the Danes, and men came flocking to join his army.

One day Hrothgar made up his mind to build a great hall with some of the spoils he had won in war. 'I had a dream,' he told his retainers, 'and in the dream I saw a hall that was bigger than any hall built since the beginning of the world. The floors shone, and the roofs were gold. There was ivory everywhere, and a throne where a king could sit. Just such a place I am going to make. Poets will sing in it – of fights and wounds and the might of my great-grandfather, Scyld Scefing. And my own brave men will eat and drink in it. I shall call the hall Heorot.'

Stone for the building of the hall Heorot came from all over the world. The masons planned, and the diggers dug down so that it was founded on rock. The banging of hammers and chink of chisels filled the air, summer, autumn, winter, and spring. It looked like a sleeping giant covered with ants as the builders went about their task.

At last Heorot was finished. It stood tall and firm on the edge of the misty fen. By day, it towered above men's heads like a second sun, so bright were its walls and roofs. By night, the torchlight blazing from its high windows, it was like a huge sentinel who did not sleep. Everyone agreed that the king had built a wonder.

Hrothgar said: 'I am pleased. My dream has come true.' And he sent out messengers inviting the most noble lords in the land to come to a banquet to celebrate the opening of Heorot's doors.

Poets sang at the feast, and the guests had so much to eat and drink that some of them could hardly walk. Hrothgar gave every man present a ring from his treasury. The music of the harp and the happy shouting of the warriors echoed out across the dark fen and drowned the crying of birds that flew in the night.

The banquet over, the guests retired to sleep. Hrothgar had had sleeping chambers built for the most important ones, far away from the smoke and bustle of the kitchens, with great curved couches comfortably heaped with skins. Only the king's bodyguard, thirty of his toughest fighting men, remained in the hall itself. They were supposed to keep awake and watch for enemies, but, as it turned out, they were all so weary from the feast that they soon slept too. They satisfied their consciences with the thought that Hrothgar was now so strong a ruler that no one would dare to attack him. Soon hall Heorot was a palace of snores.

Out in the black fen something stirred. It was cruel and slimy and its eyes shone green. A part of the night it moved through, its wicked heart was darker than the darkest place in that night. Even the moon would not look at it.

A trail of blood was left on the mud where the creature crawled. This was because it fed on living things and had grown so fat and swollen in its greed that bits of the people it had eaten dripped from its scummy lips and crooked teeth. Its claws were red and its breath, coming in little gasps, stank like a drain.

The fen was full of evil things that feared the light. There were vampires and witches and ogres and worms that burned. Horses with no heads and with hands instead of hooves loomed out of the fog. Black bats flew there, with wings like coffin-lids. Rats as big as dogs swarmed about in packs, killing and eating anything that got in their way. Some of the pools were so thick and dreggy that no one knew what lurked in the bottom of them. A few were bottomless, and went straight down to hell.

It was from the darkest of these pools that the creature with green eyes had come. It was chief of all the horrors of the fen, and even the angry rats turned tail and fled when they saw its grisly head emerging. Now it made a noise in its throat like the crunching of bones or the sudden fracture of ice underfoot.

A bat shrieked.

'Grendel,' hissed the warning wind in the grasses. 'Grendel, Grendel, Grendel!'

The creature Grendel dragged himself towards hall Heorot.

Morning came. The sun shone. The birds began to sing.

Hrothgar woke up bathed in sweat from a terrible dream. 'My hall,' he cried, 'my lovely hall was full of blood!'

His servants tried to comfort him. 'It was only a dream, master. You ate cheese before retiring for the night. Bad dreams mean cheese, nothing more.'

But the king would not be comforted. He held his head in his hands and turned his face to the wall.

'Go down into the hall,' he said at last. 'Go down and see the worst, and then come back and tell me what you have seen.'

Dutifully the servants did as he commanded them. They laughed and joked as they went down to the first twist of the great stair that ran through Heorot like a corkscrew. 'Hrothgar's a brave man and a good king,' said one. 'But he always was a bit superstitious.'

His companion agreed. 'Never eat cheese last thing at night,' he said. 'Not even if you've got a stomach like Scyld Scefing. Simple as that.'

Their feet echoed on the stair.

'Bit quiet, isn't it?'

'Nothing strange about that. The place is so big. Nice day, though. Hear the larks singing? Tell you what, let's take the couches out in the sun and give them a bit of an airing. Good idea?'

No answer.

The servant looked at his fellow. The first servant's face had gone white. He pointed waveringly down the stair.

Both men started shaking with fright.

There was no sign to be seen of the thirty warriors of the king's bodyguard.

And another of Hrothgar's dreams had come true. The ivory floors and walls of the great banqueting hall were dripping with blood.

3
TEN
AGAINST
GRENDEL

'It's like a slaughterhouse,' said Hrothgar. He had got over his despair. His eyes were angry and his mouth was set in a tight grim line as he watched the servants mopping and scrubbing the blood from the ivory hall.

His wife, Wealhtheow, laid her hand on his arm. 'Husband,' she said simply, 'who can have done this terrible thing?'

'I don't know,' admitted Hrothgar. 'But when I find the culprits I shall make them pay for it with blood of their own.'

Unferth, the son of Ecglaf, was standing nearby. He was a rude and drunken fellow, always ready to argue, even with the king himself. 'You'll never have revenge, great Hrothgar, mighty as you are,' he said, rather sneeringly, in a hard, dull voice.

'How's that?' demanded Hrothgar.

Unferth shrugged. His shoulders were narrow and he had a boil on his neck. He rubbed with his toe at a smudge of blood on the floor where he stood. 'Because this was no mortal deed,' he said. 'Thirty men gone in a single night, and no trace of their having offered resistance. Well, it's obvious what happened. They were eaten.'

Wealhtheow gasped. 'Eaten?' she exclaimed.

Unferth nodded. A horrid little look of amusement hovered about his mouth. 'That's right. Grendel was here!'

'I've never believed in Grendel,' the queen said slowly. 'It's just a tale to frighten children when they're naughty. "If you're not good, Grendel will come and gobble you up" – that's what my old nurse used to say.' She shivered, half-pleased by the memory. 'Besides,' she went on, 'all those stories of Grendel are very old. Nobody believes in that kind of thing any more.'

'I do,' snapped Unferth. 'Grendel is the wickedest fiend who ever crawled in darkness. He lives with the wolves and the mists. Some say that when Cain killed his brother, Abel, he ran away on all fours, howling, like a dog, and did not stop until he found a den at the end of the earth. And in that den, cast out and damned by God, Cain joined with a loathly snake, as black as jet, that drank the scum that comes on liquids bubbled up from the bowels of hell. One of their children had three heads, and vipers instead of fingers. Another was mouthed like a shark, but could fly through the air. The most hideous and evil of all was Grendel. The earth quaked at his birth, and stars pitched into the sea. He is made of hate, greedy for men's blood, the arch-enemy of all good things, the vilest – '

'All right,' said Hrothgar, 'there's no need to sound as though you enjoy it so much.'

Unferth scratched his boil with a grimy fingernail. His eyes, small and malicious, fed on Queen Wealhtheow's fear. 'Grendel did this,' he said, with sinister softness, after a long, uneasy pause during which the only sound came from the scrubbing-brushes of the servants trying to clean the blood from the walls. 'I know it.'

'I believe you do,' Hrothgar said. 'It takes an evil nose to smell the devil.'

Wealhtheow tossed her golden hair. She said: 'If it is true, and there is such a wickedness at work in the night, then who can withstand it? The fiend must be angered by the shining hall you have built, husband. The happiness of the harp, the songs of the poets, the laughter of your warriors – all this must bruise his vicious heart.'

'That's right,' sneered Unferth. 'Grendel will be back. And next time it will be worse.' He looked sideways as he spoke, as if fascinated by the prospect.

Hrothgar nodded grimly. 'Let him come,' he said. 'He will not be made welcome.'

'What will you do?' Wealhtheow asked.

'I shall wait for him,' promised Hrothgar, 'this night and every night. I shall wait for him with the nine lords who have the bravest hearts and the sharpest swords in this land of Danes. No child of Cain is going to ruin hall Heorot.'

Unferth took a swig from his drinking-horn. Aloud, he praised King Hrothgar's courage. Silently, he drank a toast to the demon Grendel.

Nine war-lords came at Hrothgar's call. They swore vengeance when they learned what had happened to the thirty warriors of the king's bodyguard. 'It was because they slept,' declared one. 'Grendel shall not catch us unawares.' All were keen that so terrible a deed should be swiftly avenged, and that no further disaster befall the great hall the king had built for them to feast in.

Swords were honed, shields polished, helmets daubed with grease so that the monster should not seize them easily to bite off their heads. Hrothgar himself wore a golden breastplate that shone in the least light. He was determined to meet Grendel face to face, because of the insult to Heorot.

Night fell. There was no moon, and the stars looked sparse and adrift in the punished sky. Queen Wealhtheow paced the corridors, wringing her white hands until the knucklebones nearly pierced the delicate flesh. Unferth, drunk, his buckle-belt undone, leaned from a turret to scan the murky marsh. Hrothgar and his lords waited in the banqueting hall below. Food was set out, steaming on the tables; but nobody felt like eating it.

The coming of Grendel was neither swift nor slow. This time, the night so thick, it was impossible to tell the precise moment when the creature emerged from his dreggy pool and began to drag his coils towards hall Heorot. There was only the sound to go by – the foul breath squeaking in little gasps, the noise in his throat like the splintery crunching of bones. The rats could not see him and ran over his scales in the dark. Grendel let them go. He was hungry for more than rats.

The door of the banqueting hall was thick and studded.

Stout bars held it shut against the night's alarms. None of the ten waiting warriors had slept a wink. Hrothgar's eyes never left the door. He sat bolt upright, sword in hand, a broad axe at his side. The others were in similar attitudes.

But they had no chance against the fury of the beast.

One moment the door was standing . . . the next, it was down, smashed by a single blow, and Grendel was upon them!

Hrothgar was not able to remember rightly what happened then, nor exactly how he managed to escape with his life. The hall was a confusion of swords and blood, the brave lords hurling themselves at Grendel, and the fiend snatching them up in his claws and snapping their backs as if they were no more than toys. Man after man went into those terrible jaws, and still Grendel came on, unsatisfied, his green eyes glaring, his slimy skin not even scratched by the hacking axes. It was as if the night itself had poured into hall Heorot, killing and eating mere men, the creatures of day. Torches went out as Grendel came past them. Soon the hall was pitch black, and the only sound the crunching and munching of bones and flesh.

High above, Queen Wealhtheow began to scream and pray. Unferth had fainted, either from fear or excitement. A burning brand he had been holding in his hand rolled down the stair. The queen caught hold of it. The flame licked at her fingers. She cried out in agony, and threw the thing down into the dark where the monster was. The brand missed Grendel, but it crashed to the floor beside the prostrate figure of Hrothgar, singeing his red hair where the great horned helmet had been knocked off.

Perhaps this saved her husband's life. His golden

breastplate shone like a holy light in all that dark. Even the baleful green of the monster's eyes seemed to dim before it.

For whatever reason, Grendel hesitated a moment.

Wealhtheow, seizing her chance, wanting to die with the man she loved, flew down the stair and flung herself on her husband's unconscious body. Her blue cloak covered him like a wing.

Thinking him dead, she kissed him and moaned his name. 'Hrothgar! My lord, my love! Hrothgar!'

Then she fainted.

When she woke, the king was still in her arms, badly wounded but alive. Her blue cloak was dark with his blood. She began to tear it up to bind his wounds. Unferth stood over them, holding the brand, with a tortured look in his eyes as if it were his own hand burning.

4
BEOWULF

Hrothgar's poets took the story of Grendel with them wherever they went. One of them told it in the court of Hygelac, king of the Geats, which lay far from the land of the Danes, over the stormy sea. He found eager listeners to his tale.

'We have heard of the great hall Heorot,' said Hygelac. 'Men say that its timbers reach up for the clouds, and that its golden roofs can be seen a day's march away, brighter than the sun itself.'

'Then men tell true,' answered the poet, 'for that is how Heorot is by day. But by night it's a different story. After darkfall the hall stands abandoned. None dare go there.'

'For fear of Grendel?'

'For fear of Grendel.'

Now, King Hygelac had a nephew, and his nephew's name was Beowulf. Beowulf was only a young man, but already he had won fame on account of his goodness and daring. In his person, Beowulf was below average size; he looked taller sitting down than standing up, because his broad chest and shoulders were out of proportion to his legs, which were short. He had straight brown hair and strong wrists. People found it difficult to say what was memorable or remarkable about his face – but all remembered it. He had a way of looking straight at the person he was talking to, his shoulders set square, his hands on his knees, his eyes unwavering, that always struck others as honest and open. And when someone spoke to him, he sat just as still and attentive, listening with his eyes.

In fact, Beowulf's eyes were not strong, and part of their sensitivity was due to his not seeing too well. As a boy, he had been fond of playing with bees – Beowulf means 'the bee-hunter' – and one day an angry swarm had attacked his face, stinging his cheeks and eyelids rather badly. Whether or not this was responsible for his short sight, who could say? But certainly the stings had been deep and painful enough to keep him in a darkened room for weeks, and when he emerged into daylight again he found things seemed more misty and distant than they had before. A setback like this did not daunt him. He did not even blame the bees. Beowulf was the rare kind of person who makes strength of his own weaknesses. His eyes being poor, he determined to see not just as well as other people, but better than most. He did this by cultivating habits of quickness and concentration that enabled him to be truly *seeing* where others were only looking. And this matter of the eyes was typical of his whole manner of being. Beowulf had made the best of all he had, putting each imperfection to work in the service of his integrity. Thus, his real strength lay in the balance of his person – which is, perhaps, another way of saying that he was strong because he was good, and good because he had the strength to accept things in him that were bad.

When Beowulf had heard all the stories about the dreadful deeds of the demon Grendel, he determined to go and help Hrothgar, if he could. His ship was made ready, a fine seaworthy craft with a great curved prow. He chose fourteen men to go with him. They were brave indomitable fellows, well tested in battle and willing to follow their hero wherever he went. However, it was not merely for their skill as warriors that Beowulf picked them. He had heard enough about Grendel to know that the monster could not be killed by strength alone.

Wind filled the sails, and the ship sped forward. The second day, they came in sight of the land of the Danes. As they were disembarking, a man came galloping along the beach towards them. He carried a long spear, and his horse kicked up a stinging shower of shingle as he drew rein.

'Halt!' he cried, his voice like thunder. 'Who are you who dare to land so brazenly on Hrothgar's coast? What do you want and why do you come bearing so many weapons? If you are pirates, then be warned by me. I have only to set this horn to my lips and sound the warning note, and you will be met by such an army that not one of you shall ever see home again!'

Beowulf nodded, tossing shells into the sea. Some of his

17

men had reached for their swords, but with an easy flick of his wrist he motioned to them to stop.

'We are no pirates,' he said. 'Who are you?'

The horseman drew himself up proudly. 'I am Hrothgar's coastguard,' he shouted. 'No one bent on mischief gets past me.'

Beowulf did not shout, but his voice sounded clear and distinct over the noisy waves and the crying of sea birds. 'I am Beowulf, son of Ecgtheow,' he said. 'I am come to do what I can against the demon Grendel.'

A shiver went down the coastguard's weather-beaten cheek. It was plain that though he was a brave man, he did not like to hear about Grendel.

Beowulf went on calmly: 'If you love your country – as I'm sure you do – then you'll help, not hinder us. Show us the way to the great hall Heorot.'

The coastguard was impressed by the quiet strength of this stranger's speaking. He thought a moment, then he said: 'I will escort you to Hrothgar himself. He can decide the seriousness of your errand. I'm just a common warrior set to guard the shores, and I can't see how your little band can stand against a fiend like Grendel.' He leaned forward confidentially in his saddle. 'If you take my private advice,' he added, 'you'll pack back in your ship before you're all killed. The man's not born who can get the better of Grendel. The king is quite resigned to it. Fighting that monster, why, it's like fighting the sea! You can't win!'

Beowulf's men muttered angrily amongst themselves. They found the coastguard's words insulting.

Beowulf did not seem insulted. He looked out over the rolling waves as though considering what the coastguard

18

had said. 'Thank you for your advice,' he said at last, 'but I will not take it.'

The coastguard shrugged. 'Then you are either the bravest man in the world or a simple fool. Get your men in marching order, and I will lead you to Heorot. Don't worry about your ship. Let it ride here at anchor, and I'll have my soldiers guard it.' He smiled grimly, wheeling his horse about. 'I shan't say they'll keep it safe for you until you come back, because I doubt very much whether you will come back, any of you, if it's really Grendel you're after.'

Beowulf's men wore coats of mail. Their helmets had golden boar-crests on them. They carried swords and ash spears tipped with iron. Armour and equipment proved heavy in the midday sun. They clanked along, uncomplaining, the sweat pouring down their faces, in single file behind the coastguard's horse. Beowulf looked about him as he marched, taking everything in, tall cliffs and deep valleys, each tumbling stream and pebble winking brightly in the sun. His head moved on his shoulders like a bird's: alert, inquisitive, shrewd.

Before long they came in sight of Heorot. The shining of the place astonished them. It stood like a tower of solid gold. Beyond it, shrouded in mist even on a day like this, lay the fen.

To Beowulf – perhaps because of his short sight – hall Heorot appeared even brighter than it was, and the badlands darker. He stood on a grassy mound gazing down at the gold and the black for a long while, until his men began to grow restless and the coastguard's horse flared its nostrils wide, impatient to be back within smelling distance of the sea.

Then Beowulf thanked the coastguard for showing them the way, and led his men along the winding stone road to Heorot. The coastguard watched them go, thinking how brave and doomed they looked, until they were so far away that he could no longer hear the clinking of their armour. He saw that Beowulf had left his sword stuck in the top of the mound. It shone in the sunlight like a cross.

5
NINE SEA-MONSTERS

Hrothgar's hair, once red as fire, had turned white with worry about Grendel. His heart was sickened by slaughter. So many men had waited in hall Heorot to face the fiend, and been eaten for their courage, that the king had come to think he was being punished for his pride in building such a magnificence. He rested his jutting jaw on his hand, and welcomed Beowulf without much confidence.

'I knew your father,' he said, after they had exchanged salutes. 'He was a tall, strong man, with an eye like a hawk's.'

Beowulf blinked and smiled. 'Great Hrothgar,' he said politely, 'I am not tall, as you see, and my enemies liken my eyes to the bat's. But the bat knows well enough where he is going in the night, and so do I.'

Hrothgar shook his head slowly, as though it buzzed

with sorrow. 'I suppose you have come to fight Grendel,' he muttered. 'Please go home again. There's nothing anyone can do.'

Beowulf sat down on the steps by the king's throne. His manner was relaxed and easy. Hrothgar could not help liking this plain young man – there was such an air of simplicity about him. He shuddered and touched the scars on his own face – livid marks made by Grendel's claws – as he thought what the monster would do to that simplicity.

Beowulf was eating an apple. He bit into it with cheerful determination. The tips of his fingers were square-shaped. Hrothgar noticed how strong his wrists were.

Beowulf said: 'These apples are good. Do you want one?'

'Where do they grow?'

'In the valley on the other side of the hill. I had my men pick a sackful as we marched past.' Beowulf nodded to one of his followers. The man chose an apple from a huge bag he had been carrying on his back, and brought it to the king. Hrothgar balanced it on the palm of his hand and considered it doubtfully.

'That grove is witch-work,' he said, looking at Beowulf as though he expected him to be turned into a pig at any minute.

Unferth, slouched over a cup, rich mead sticky in his whiskers, grinned agreement. 'An old witch spat her teeth out there,' he muttered. 'They were bad teeth – green and red and rotting. They grew into apple trees. Nobody in his right mind would eat fruit like that.'

Beowulf took a big bite and finished his apple, pips, core, and all.

'You feel well?' asked the king.

'Never better.'

'But you heard what Unferth said?'

'I heard.'

Unferth scowled, and poked at his boil. 'Only someone wicked could eat witch's apples and come to no harm,' he insinuated darkly.

Beowulf laughed. Hrothgar thought that it was a long time since he had heard such a free and easy sound in hall Heorot.

'I don't like being laughed at,' whined Unferth, drawing his dagger.

Beowulf swiftly handed him an apple. 'I don't peel them myself,' he said. 'Things seem to lose something with their skins off, don't you think? But every man to his own taste.'

Unferth skewered the apple with his blade. Hrothgar and Queen Wealhtheow were smiling at his discomfiture. Some of the Geats guffawed, delighted by their leader's quick wit. The Danes laughed too. Unferth was unpopular, and they liked the way this mild-tempered stranger had put him in his place. Unferth could not stand it. He sliced the apple in two and kicked the pieces away. 'I say again what I said before,' he hissed. 'The apples are bad, and only a bad –'

'The apples are good,' broke in Beowulf, his voice calm but firm. 'Listen, Unferth, and I will tell you something. You think that bad brings forth bad only, and that the good man should hold apart from it. I suggest that things aren't so simple, so black and white. Even the wickedest person can do good for someone. The truly good man finds good where he can.'

'Oh, so you're truly good, are you?' sneered Unferth.

'Not at all,' said Beowulf. 'Bad teeth don't belong only to witches. I have some myself.' He opened his mouth and pointed.

Unferth sniggered. 'Riddled with rot,' he said. 'And your teeth have obviously infected your tongue. Riddles and rot, that's what your talk is!'

Queen Wealhtheow leaned forward. Her fair hair trembled with gold in the sunlight that streamed through the hall from a high window. 'I don't think the stranger talks in riddles,' she said. 'What he says and does makes perfect sense to me.'

'Explain,' said the king patiently, still rolling his apple in his hands.

'Well,' said Wealhtheow, 'I think that Beowulf is trying to show us that in order to overcome evil, we have to admit to a little bit of it in ourselves. He can eat the witch's apple and come to no harm, because he has sufficient strength of character to find the good in it.'

'Strength?' scoffed Unferth. 'Bat's eyes and rat's teeth!'

'Quite so,' said Wealhtheow. 'He admits to his weaknesses and in the admitting they become strengths. This is no usual kind of hero.'

Hrothgar nodded thoughtfully. 'I'm inclined to agree with you, my love, although reasoning things out isn't my best point, and I can't pretend to have understood all this apple business as readily as you have.'

'Never mind understanding,' the queen said, her blue eyes patient. 'Just eat your own apple. I'm sure it's tasty.'

Hrothgar crossed himself. And took a bite. Everyone

watched him expectantly. He took another bite. He chewed. He swallowed. He could not help thinking of the witch, but neither could he help admitting that the apple was delicious. 'It's fine and ripe,' he said at last, smacking his lips. 'Neither too sour nor too sweet.'

Beowulf beamed. He said: 'Now, about Grendel –'

'Wait a bit,' snapped Unferth. 'What about Breca?'

'Breca?' said Hrothgar. 'Who's Breca?'

Unferth's thin lips were wry and ugly with malice. 'Breca,' he said slowly, savouring each nasty word, 'was the name of a friend of our fine hero here. I just remembered the story while you and the queen were busy heaping incomprehensible praises on him. Not a pretty story, is it, Beowulf? You tried to drown your friend because he was a better swimmer than you!'

After Unferth's outburst some of the Geats wanted to throttle him, they were so furious at this insult to their leader. But Beowulf walked among them coolly, advising restraint. Hrothgar shifted about uneasily on his throne, glaring at Unferth, wanting to apologize to Beowulf for his henchman's uncouth behaviour. But Queen Wealhtheow caught at his sleeve and whispered to him to wait and see what Beowulf had to say. 'It's a kind of test,' she murmured behind her hand. 'So far everything has gone the stranger's way. Let's watch how he deals with this.'

Beowulf came and stood before them. His face was pale. His eyes had a faraway look. He spoke with a straightforward seriousness that made everyone fall silent. His voice echoed compellingly in the hushed hall.

'Mighty Hrothgar, wise Wealhtheow,' Beowulf said, 'the truth is not as your man Unferth has told it. What happened was this. When I was a boy, I had a friend called Breca. We both loved swimming. We used to go out together and wrestle with the waves, whatever the weather. One day we made a dare with each other, as boys will. The dare was that each of us was to enter the sea, sword in hand, and keep swimming until one gave up.' Beowulf smiled, as though all this struck him as great foolishness now. 'If you ask me why we took swords,' he went on, 'I can only say that we had some conceited idea of fighting whales with them. Anyway, we were both good swimmers, and we went on and on, for five days and five nights, neither willing to admit defeat, until a terrible storm drove us apart. I'll never forget that moment. The sky grew dark at noon, and the wind lashed the sea until it boiled. The creatures of the deep were driven mad by the storm. Something caught hold of me – to this day, I'm not sure whether it was the furious sea-swell or some monster from the ocean-bed – and dragged me towards the rocks at the foot of cliffs, which suddenly loomed up from nowhere. I clung on hard. I turned to face the roaring waves. And then monsters did indeed appear. Nine of them, one after another, sliding slick with jaws agape through the heaving sea. And I swung my sword about my head and fought them off. I killed them. Nine sea-monsters. I killed them. The wind stopped. The waves dropped. I was on Lapland shore, exhausted, covered in seaweed, and I slept. As for Breca, he was not drowned. The current swept him to Norway. He was a better swimmer than I.'

The Geats burst out cheering as Beowulf finished. They had heard the story before, of course, but never so plainly from Beowulf's lips. He was not given to boasting, and had offered his account simply as an answer to Unferth's lie.

King Hrothgar was stirred by the telling of such brave deeds. He was a warrior at heart, and here was something he could easily understand and appreciate. He commanded his servants to prepare a banquet fit for a hero. The feasting and drinking went on for hours. Only Unferth did not join in. He sat in a corner, picking moodily at his boil, glaring at the bright assembled company.

Long shadows crept into hall Heorot. Night was coming on. Some of the Danes grew restless and apprehensive. They did not like to show their fear of Grendel, but their hands quivered where they held the drinking-horns, and their eyes kept returning to the door.

Hrothgar consulted with Wealhtheow. Then he said to Beowulf: 'You are determined to face Grendel, come what may?'

'I am,' said Beowulf quietly.

'What is your plan?'

'The best plan,' said Beowulf. 'No plan.'

Hrothgar shook his head. 'You are the bravest man I have ever met,' he said, standing up to salute his guest. 'If anyone can kill Grendel, it is you.' He suddenly noticed something about Beowulf that had escaped his attention before. 'Where is your sword?' he asked.

Beowulf shrugged. 'My sword? Oh, I left it in the sun somewhere. I need no sword.'

'No sword! But how – ?'

'Does Grendel use a sword?' demanded Beowulf.

'Of course not. But he will eat –'

'Have swords been any good against him in the past?' Beowulf pursued relentlessly.

Hrothgar had to admit that they had not. But he could not see how one man, however good and strong, dared face the fiend without weapons.

Beowulf held up his hands. 'Here are weapons enough,' he said. 'I put more trust in these ten fingers than in a hundred swords.'

Hrothgar wanted to argue. He was desperately worried now. He thought Beowulf mad. He thought it was suicide to wait for Grendel – Grendel the murderously all-powerful – without at least a good keen blade for company. What could one man's hands hope to do to that black terror?

Queen Wealhtheow silenced her husband's objections. She brought the banquet to a close by giving Beowulf a golden cup to drink from.

Beowulf drank deep, his eyes not leaving hers.

He handed the cup back to her and smiled as though he had taken sustenance from the deepest well in the world.

Then, as the Danes were about to leave, the night already rustling at hall Heorot's doors, Unferth surprised them all, and perhaps himself, by saying: 'I am going to stay. I want to see what happens when this fool tries to shake hands with Grendel.'

6
BEOWULF
AGAINST
GRENDEL

Beowulf's men were weary and soon slept. They lay stretched out on couches all round the hall. Their sea voyaging, followed by the march to Heorot and the many cups of mead Hrothgar had given them, made them sleep deep. Only Beowulf and Unferth stayed awake. They sat on either side of the empty throne, watching for Grendel's coming.

Unferth played with a silver trinket. He kept pouring the little chain through his fingers, its links making a tinkling sound. Sometimes he drew it so tight about his wrist that it hurt. He smiled to himself in the dark. He had stopped drinking. He was afraid, but his fear fascinated him. His bladder ached; he wanted to make water; but he did not dare go out in the night to do so. He twisted about on the hard, uncomfortable step. He could feel the sweat trickling out of his hair.

Beowulf sat still.

It was a long night. It wore on slowly. The torches burned low. One of the Geats cried out in a bad dream. He woke, saw his leader's face, and turned back to sleep again. A torch sputtered and went out.

Beowulf could see well in half-light. He did not blink or shut his eyes. Once he cracked his knuckles. Otherwise he just watched, and waited. There was no sign of Grendel.

Unferth began gnawing at his fingernails. They tasted of dirt and where he had been poking at his boil. Unferth hated the taste of himself, but he had to have it.

Beowulf still sat still.

Then, as dawn began to drain the dark, both men heard a sound. Beowulf heard it first. It was a sound like the breaking of ice underfoot. It came quick and was gone again. Unferth shook his head, wondering if he had imagined it. Then there was a hissing, gasping, panting noise outside the door, swiftly stifled, as though someone – or some Thing – was holding his breath in the dark, waiting to pounce.

Again there came that splintery sound.

Unferth's blood ran cold. He cowered into shadow. He felt his own water leaking down his leg, sore and warm and sticky.

Beowulf stood up. His voice rang through the raftered hall.

'Grendel,' he cried, 'Grendel, child of Cain, come down into Heorot. I am Beowulf, son of Ecgtheow. I am Beowulf, not afraid of you. I am Beowulf, come to kill you!'

The monster squealed with rage. His throat was full

of the noise of crunching bones. He scrabbled at the door. He tore it down with his talons. He fell into hall Heorot!

The first thing Beowulf noticed was the smell. It hit him like a great wave of rotting matter: rank, malignant, bringing tears to his eyes and making him cough. It filled the hall like a poison gas. He retched at the stink of the beast.

It was because Grendel was so huge and black that the smell came before anything the eyes could make out. He was a foul fog, a choking murk of evil vapours, looming and slithering on the ivory floor. Then Beowulf saw coil after coil of slimy skin, mucid, spongy, dripping with the filth of the swamps, smeared thick with blood and scum, maggoty, putrid, and a pair of eyes glaring green, and slobbering lips, and huge claws reaching . . .

Before Beowulf could move, those claws snatched up one of the warriors stirring out of sleep.

Grendel tore his victim limb from limb, picking off arms and legs, lapping up the blood with a greedy tongue, taking big bites to crunch up bones and swallow gory mouthfuls of flesh. In a minute all that was left of the man was a frayed mess of veins and entrails hanging from the monster's mouth.

Unferth was being sick. The green eyes flickered in his direction. He screamed, and scratched at the wall for a hiding place, but there was none. Two torches went out as Grendel slithered past them.

The hall was left completely in darkness save for some inklings of dawn at the smashed door and where the windows were. The Geats jumped up in panic and fought with each other trying to find their swords and spears.

31

Grendel made a new noise above the uproar. He gurgled bloodily with glee. The dark was his den, his home, his proper habit. He hated light. The hall shook to its foundations with his terrible laughter. He groped for Unferth.

But all at once the light had caught him. It had him by the claw. It was Beowulf!

The creature gave a dreadful squeal as Beowulf touched him. Ten strong fingers locked about his hairy wrist. To Grendel, it was as if the sun itself had caught him in its clutch. Made of wickedness as he was, the good in this man burned him. The mortal fingers were like ten red-hot nails driven into his skin. Grendel had never known strength like this. He roared and shook to be free, to crawl away, to escape into the ruins of the night. But Beowulf would not let him go.

Now Beowulf began to talk. His voice was quiet, and there was hullabaloo in the hall, what with the soldiers rushing about confusedly in the dark, and Unferth screaming and the monster threshing about to get loose – yet Grendel heard every word like thunder in his brain. He did not know what was worse: Beowulf's grip or what Beowulf said.

Beowulf said: 'Light holds you, Grendel. Light has you in its power. You, who have shunned the sun, meet me, once stung by bees that drank the sun. There's honey in my veins, Grendel, a liquid sunlight that can kill you quite. These fingers that you feel are ten great stars. Stars have no fear. I do not fear you, Grendel. I do not fear, therefore I do not fight. I only hold you, child of Cain. I only fix you fast in your own evil, so that you cannot turn it out on any other. It is your own evil, Grendel, that undoes you. You must die, creature of night, because the light has got you in a last embrace.'

Grendel was in a fury. He bellowed and lashed. He wanted above all else to get away from this thing that was so contrary to himself. He tried every vicious trick he knew. But Beowulf stood firm, holding the monster in a grip so tight that it almost made his own big fingers crack and the bones poke out of the straining flesh. Hall Heorot rocked down to its stone roots with the rage of the demon's struggling.

Somewhere deep in Grendel's hellish heart a memory stirred. It grew and spread and flooded his whole being with despair. Something to do with light and another of these children of day – one who had flung herself between him and his food, and by her love had thwarted him, so that he had felt powerless to approach and had slunk away, abashed by mystery. Grendel did not know the word 'love' or the word 'good'. To him, they were part of the light he hated. There had been such light about that woman in the blue cloak. He had had to get away from it. But the light in the woman was as nothing to the light in this man Beowulf. And try as he would, he could not get away.

Grendel grew angrier and angrier. He shook his arm about and dashed it against the wall. Beowulf, badly bruised, refused to relinquish his hold. When shaking did not work, and banging did not work, Grendel tried jerking his arm. But Beowulf wound his own legs round a pillar. He took the full force of the monster's pull – and still held on.

There was a fearful snapping of bones and tearing of sinews and muscles.

Then hot stinking blood fountained everywhere.

Beowulf had pulled Grendel's arm out of its socket!

7
CELEBRATIONS

The monster howled. It was a pandemonium of pain, as though all the men he had eaten cried out too. He dragged himself along the ivory floor, blood pumping from his wound with each fierce beat of his angry heart. He knew he must die from loss of blood.

Beowulf let Grendel go. He listened to that hideous howling dying away across the fen. The light grew stronger. The sun lit all the windows of hall Heorot.

Beowulf's men crowded round him. It was some little time before they realized the full extent of their hero's victory. Beowulf was bruised and bloody, and his cheeks were thick with slime off the monster's body. But when he hung Grendel's torn-out arm from a hook in the rafters, all the Geats burst out cheering. It was foul and green and scaly, with a tangle of blood-soaked hair at the wrist, and sharp claws where the fingers should have been. Nobody liked to touch it, but everyone looked.

Beowulf acknowledged the congratulations wearily. He called for water. It was brought. He washed the blood and dirt from his body, and combed his hair. Then he went to Unferth.

Unferth, alone, ignored, skulked under the great throne. His teeth were chattering, his eyes went to and fro, he kept trying to drink from an empty horn. But when Beowulf laid a friendly hand on his shoulder, to comfort him, he turned and snapped at it like a wolf.

'Murder!' he snarled. 'You killed him! He was beautiful, and you killed him!' And he began to sob and rock, cradling his knees in his hands.

The astonished Geats roared disapproval. 'Beautiful! He says the beast was beautiful!' Some of them wanted to take ungrateful Unferth out and hang him from the nearest tree. But Beowulf told them to leave the wretch to himself.

'To Unferth, Grendel *was* beautiful,' was all he would say when his men asked him why.

'Here comes Hrothgar,' called one by the ruined door.

The king could not believe what Beowulf had done. He stood in Heorot and stared at the terrible trophy, Grendel's arm, which still dripped steaming blood on the ivory floor.

As for Wealhtheow, she came to Beowulf with open arms and tears in her sky-blue eyes. He knelt before her, and she kissed him tenderly on the forehead.

The sun seemed to dance over the land of the Danes. An exultation of larks rose from the fen itself. They went

36

up, up, up, trilling dew from their wings, and busily rested, and sang, and sang.

King Hrothgar clapped his hands. 'Clean the hall!' he shoulted to his servants. 'Scrub the tables! Polish the benches! Hang the walls with the richest tapestries! Bring meat and mead enough for a man as strong as a hundred men! All this for Beowulf! Honour to Beowulf! Long live Beowulf, who has freed us from the monster Grendel!'

They raced their horses. They made poems and songs. They told stories of all the heroes that ever lived, and said their deeds were small compared with what brave Beowulf had done in a single night. Hrothgar gave Beowulf gifts, and the gifts were these: a banner of gold, a helmet that would not break, a sword as sharp as a flame. He also made him a present of eight of his swiftest horses, each horse decked with a golden bridle and a saddle encrusted with precious stones. And Wealhtheow gave Beowulf a ring of the purest gold to wear on his finger, and a golden collar to carry about his neck. This collar, some say, was called Brisingamen and was the most perfect thing in the world.

The feasting went on for three days and three nights. Only Unferth held apart from it, sitting in a dark corner, twisting his cloak in his hands, muttering of Grendel's 'beauty', and prophesying doom. Nobody paid any attention to him. Once, Beowulf offered him a drink. But Unferth spat it out. 'I want blood,' he said.

Of the stories told by Hrothgar's poets, all in honour of Beowulf's feat and meant to provide comparisons with what he had done, the one that made the deepest mark on

Beowulf's mind was the story of Sigemund and the Fire Dragon. This is how it went.

Long ago there was a prince called Sigemund who was a great hero. He was strong as a bear and tall as a mountain tree. He could snap chains round his chest simply by taking a big breath, and bend iron bars that it took two men to lift. Because he used his giant strength only in the service of good, he was always a very popular man. Everyone loved him.

None loved Sigemund more than his loyal nephew, Fitela. Fitela was as unlike his uncle as it is possible for two men to be. He was small in stature, timorous and shy by nature. Men said that Fitela would run away from his own shadow if Sigemund was not with him. However, this never happened, because Sigemund always was with him; the two of them were inseparable; they fought together, drank together, prayed together. You never saw huge Sigemund but you saw little Fitela, taking six strides to keep up with his uncle's one, peering askance at murky places, tugging at the giant's sleeves and offering him all sorts of useless advice in a high, squeaky voice.

Together they performed many brave deeds. Nor was puny Fitela as good-for-nothing in battle as you might think. He could skip through an enemy's legs and trip him up in a trice, while the man was still concentrating on Sigemund as his only opponent. He could hang on to horses' tails and make them rear, tumbling their riders to the ground, where it was easy enough for Sigemund to finish them off. He had great value as an impish wreaker of havoc in a line of hostile soldiers, for he had only to hop about in front of them, pulling faces, and then race round the back and shout a few names – 'Milk-chops!

Skellybum! Barmysword! Hey, you with the woolly eyebrows growing out of your ears!' – to reduce the most well-disciplined squad to an angry confusion that left them with no chance as soon as Sigemund came on the scene. In any kind of adventure Sigemund and Fitela thus proved themselves an unbeatable pair.

The killing of the Fire Dragon was an exploit that called for the best of their cunning. The Dragon was guardian of a treasure hoard so vast and valuable that they knew it would bring prosperity to their land for generations to come. For this reason they determined to slay it and take the treasure if they could.

Now, the Fire Dragon lived on an island of silver rock. It had four heads. The first head, as white as snow, breathed out air. The second head, which was black as pitch, coughed up earth. The third head, sea-green, was more terrible than either of these: it spat out great quantities of water. The fourth head was the most horrible head of all. It was flame-coloured, with bulging blood-red eyes. This head could spit out long forks of searing fire, burning everything to cinders within a range of about half a mile. Nothing grew on Silver Rock island because the Dragon hated trees and flowers and as soon as the least green shoot appeared anywhere, he would turn his fourth head to glare at it and – *whoosh! cccrrraaak!* – fry it to bits in one of his tremendous fire-spits.

Sigemund and Fitela had to work out a plan to get near the Dragon in the first place. They did it at night, swimming under water, approaching Silver Rock island from different directions. Sigemund swam slowly, stopping every now and again to surface and lie on his back, sending tall spirtles of water up out of the waves. The Fire

Dragon – which slept only three heads at a time, so that one pair of eyes was always on the look-out – thought it was just a whale playing in the moonlight, and took no notice. Meanwhile, Fitela had reached the rock from the north. Being so small, he was able to crawl up behind the Dragon without being seen. Sigemund dived down to the sea-bed again and swam quickly towards the island.

Little Fitela was crouched right by the Dragon's tail. As soon as he saw big telltale bubbles indicating that his uncle was about to emerge from the sea, he grabbed the tail boldly in both hands – and twisted it as hard as he could!

The Dragon roared with anger.

It turned its terrible fourth head to see and destroy whatever the impudent thing was that dared to tweak its tail. It was astonished by Fitela's smallness.

Sigemund took good advantage of that moment of astonishment. He heaved himself up on the silver rock and hurled himself at the Dragon. The head that breathed out air lunged at him. Sigemund seized it by the throat and twisted it round. Air came hissing from the head just as fire began to fork from the other one. Fitela would have been burned alive if the flames had reached him. But they did not reach him. Sigemund had locked the two heads together, so that the fire was beaten back down the Dragon's windpipe by the blast of air from its other mouth. It writhed and coughed. Fitela pulled again at its tail. Again, the Dragon tried to get its fire-throwing head in position to deal with him. But Sigemund grabbed another head, the black one, already coughing up cart-loads of earth, and bent the tough neck in his powerful hands, ramming it into the jaws where fire struggled to get the better of air. Dark heavy soil poured down the Dragon's throat. His red eyes popped out of his head as he choked on it.

Fitela twisted the Dragon's tail once more. Sigemund added the water-squirting head to the complicated knot he had already made out of the Dragon's three other heads. The forks of flame, met by air, earth, and a great flood of water, had no chance to get out. The fire travelled down into the Dragon's belly. He gave a fearful belch, and died.

In this way, Sigemund and Fitela won the Fire Dragon's treasure hoard for the good of their people. When they looked in the cave that had been his den, they found it was crammed to the roof with gold and silver and diamonds and rubies and pearls. They loaded ten ships with their plunder, and sailed happily home.

After this cunning adventure, the storyteller concluded, Sigemund and Fitela were famous the whole world over. 'But their deeds were as flea-bites compared to Beowulf's,' he added, putting down his harp.

Beowulf laughed. He was amused and pleased by this tale, and stored it in his memory.

Queen Wealhtheow poured the last of the wine into another golden cup for him to drink from.

Hrothgar had fallen asleep on his throne, his white-haired head against his polished shield.

Soon all the lords and warriors followed suit. They were worn out with happiness. Danes and Geats sprawled side by side on the long straight benches of the banqueting hall, content that Heorot was a safe place now, well satisfied with the celebrations they had had in the hero's honour. The poets snored, sore-throated from so much storytelling. The servants dreamt of being masters.

Beowulf slept too, his head on his hands, the golden collar glittering round his neck.

Only Unferth remained awake. He stared at the arm, which hung from the hook. His eyes were dry and bloodshot, full of black thoughts.

8
REVENGE

In the heart of the night, in the darkest dark of the darkness, something stirred from the fen. It was shaped like a snake, a snake as black as jet, long and fat and hissing, but it moved across the marshy ground faster than any snake that ever was, because it had tentacles that pulled it through the mud as quick and slick as a knife going through butter. Its flesh was greasy. It had red lips and hanging breasts. It dribbled green bile and gobbets of blood.

The wind in the grasses, which had whispered at Grendel's coming, held its breath icily as this new horror slithered on towards hall Heorot. The rats ran away, tails lashing, eyes blind with panic. The owls forgot to ask their *Who? Who? Who?*

The creatures of the fen knew who – and they were frightened.

A long, long time ago She had come from Her bottomless pool to join with the murderer Cain. The fen shook then with unnatural storms as it witnessed their loathsome embracings. The moon dripped blood, and the strict stars collided in their courses. A bolt of lightning struck Cain dead for the horror of what he had done. But She lived on. She was too much a part of death to ever die. She was neither older nor younger than She had been in the beginning. What She was could never be destroyed.

A werewolf howled on a crag.

A cloud of white vampire moths hovered above Her grisly head.

She had no name.

She was She, She, She . . .

Grendel's Mother!

Unferth knew.

Unferth knew that Something was coming.

Not even his boil or his silver trinket or his long black cloak could comfort his hands this time. They twitched with a life of their own. His thumbs pricked. His fingers itched. The veins in his sweaty palms were hard and swollen and painful.

Half-moaning, half-humming, he sat and watched the sleepers in the hall. He despised them all. Stupid Hrothgar, he thought, murderous Beowulf. They were only people, silly creatures of flesh and blood, mortal trash. He hated them.

Unferth longed for he knew not what. Something vast and dark and terrible. Something that would recognize him as a cut above the merely human. Something that would press him to Its hideous heart and make him welcome as Its own.

He was terribly alone. He did not belong here, in the torchlit hall littered with cups and harps, the debris of celebrations he had taken no part in. He belonged out there in the night, the fatal darkness, the imperishable black. For day, he thought, did not really kill the dark. It was always there, out there in the fen, living on in the veins of the children of Cain. Beowulf believed he could put a stop to it simply by slaying one monster. What a fool! He, Unferth, knew better, knew that good and evil were locked in such an endless contest that the death of just one of the powers of darkness was of no significance whatsoever. As well believe you could destroy a tree by tearing off a single leaf!

And the tree of evil looked taller and more familiar to Unferth than the slender green tree of good. Its twisted roots went down into his own being. He could feel its festering sap in every fibre of him. Even his boil, he reasoned, was an outward mark of his difference from such as Beowulf. If only Grendel had understood . . .

But Grendel had not understood. Grendel had tried to kill him. Why?

Unferth slapped his side as a sudden illumination came into the dark chamber of his thought.

It was not Grendel who had misunderstood. It was himself. Grendel had wanted to take him for his own, to bear him off to where he belonged, to join the baleful company of the fen; but he, Unferth, had held back through fear. All at once he hated his fear – the sweat on his cheeks that proved him weak and human, the trembling of his hands that measured the distance between him and Grendel, all the frailties of his humble mortal state.

Unferth stared at his own flesh with a bad taste in his mouth. It seemed an unwarrantable interference, something that held his lovely capacity for evil behind bars. If only he could strip it off, be free of it, live solely and for ever as a sort of cruel essential ghost or demon of himself . . . If only, if only . . .

Unferth gnawed at his knuckles like an animal trying to rid itself of a wounded and unwanted limb.

He was very near to madness in that night.

She came into hall Heorot.
She made no noise.
She looked at Unferth and She smiled.
Her lips were red.
She had eyes in Her breasts.
Unferth stood up and stretched out his arms.
'Welcome,' he said.

Wealhtheow woke first. On the edge of sleep, she had dreamt of a sow eating her farrow. She opened her eyes and saw that Grendel's arm was gone from the hook in the rafters.

She woke the king, and Beowulf too. Both shook their heads, as if to clear them of bad dreams.

Beowulf said: 'It seems we slept deep.'

'Too deep for safekeeping,' said Wealhtheow. 'Grendel's arm has been stolen by some thief in the night.'

Hrothgar started up with a shout. 'That's not the worst of it!' he cried. 'Look, there, by the golden tapestry! Oh, Aeschere! Aeschere!'

A man's body lay, face to the wall, on the ivory floor. He had a dagger in his back. He was dead.

Beowulf bent over him.

'It is Aeschere,' said Hrothgar broken-heartedly. Tears glistened on his cheeks and in the winter whiteness of his beard. His jutting jaw went slack with sorrow. 'Aeschere! My best friend, dearer to me than my own hand. We were boys together. We went to war together. A splendid man – his mind as sharp as his sword. I loved him. He is dead. Only Grendel could have done this.'

Beowulf was peering at the dagger between Aeschere's shoulder blades. 'I have seen this hilt before,' he said. 'This is the dagger Unferth drew on me.'

'Unferth! Unferth killed Aeschere while he slept! Why? Why?'

'There is no why where Unferth is concerned,' said Beowulf. 'He acts as a beast would, blindly. He's at the mercy of his own evil, and hardly knows what he does.'

'He shall die for this!' vowed Hrothgar. 'Guards! Guards! Find the vile, treacherous coward Unferth in whatever dark corner he is hiding, and bring him straight to me!'

But Unferth was not to be found. Danes and Geats searched everywhere, to no avail. All they discovered was a strange, sweet-smelling spoor that led twistingly into the fen.

Beowulf said: 'This much is clear – Aeschere is dead; Unferth is gone; Grendel's arm has been stolen. Now, Unferth probably murdered Aeschere. It is his dagger, and the deed looks like him. But it's unlikely we'll ever know for certain because –'

'What do you mean?' cried Hrothgar, eyes bright for

vengeance. 'We will find Unferth and torture the wretch until he confesses! He's out there in the fen somewhere, drooling over the monster's arm, mad and bad and –'

'I was coming to that,' Beowulf explained patiently. 'I don't think Unferth took Grendel's arm. His wrists weren't strong enough to lift it down without dropping it and wakening us all. He was a weakling, in more ways than one.'

Wealhtheow said: 'You speak of him as though he were dead.'

'I shall be surprised if he is not,' said Beowulf. 'There is the matter of the spoor, you see. Something came out of the fen for Grendel's arm, and whatever it was that came took Unferth too.'

'And killed him?' asked Hrothgar eagerly. 'He deserved it.'

'Perhaps,' said Beowulf.

Wealhtheow sighed, distressed by so much horror. 'What do you think it was, the creature? Grendel?'

Beowulf shook his head. 'Grendel had no might left. I broke more than his arm. He is surely dead.'

'Then who?' demanded the king. He was desperate to set out in search of someone or something in order to avenge poor Aeschere.

'I do not know this country,' said Beowulf. 'Perhaps you can tell me of other monsters who are known to haunt the fen? Something that moves in a twisty way, like a snake, and leaves a spoor that smells as sweet as mother's milk?'

Hrothgar frowned, and confessed himself at his wit's end.

48

'Something sly and noiseless,' prompted Beowulf. 'Something more terrible than Grendel.'

Wealhtheow caught her breath. She had remembered the stories of her childhood, the most loathly and ancient bugaboo her nurse had ever frightened her with. And at the same time she remembered Unferth's fascinated talking on this subject, here, in the very hall where they now stood.

Beowulf looked at her keenly. 'Yes?' he said.

'There is only one thing it can be,' said Wealhtheow. 'She has no name.'

'Perhaps she is too horrible for people to want to name her?'

'Just so,' said Wealhtheow. 'She is Grendel's Mother!'

9
INTO
THE
FEN

The fen was wild and waste. It stretched as far as the eye could see. The sky over it was grey. The sun was bleak and sere. It was a dead land.

Beowulf rode on one of the horses Hrothgar had given him. It was white, with a black mane. He picked his way slowly, following the spoor. His men followed him.

He had never before been in so desolate a place. The wind was thin and moaning in the reeds. Birds did not sing. Even the light had a brief look about it, as though it were a trespasser.

Beowulf wore a blue cloak and the golden collar Queen Wealhtheow had given him. On his head was the helmet that would not break, at his side the sword as sharp as a flame. However, he did not put his trust in these. He knew that for Grendel's Mother, as for Grendel, more

50

subtle and essential weapons were necessary. Beowulf's best weapon was himself. He put all his faith in that.

Wealhtheow had not begged him not to go. She knew he must. Hrothgar had wanted to come too, he was so incensed by the wanton slaying of Aeschere. But Beowulf told him to stay in Heorot. 'A king's place is with his people. Besides, if I fail – as I might against such a she-devil – who would there be to protect this land of Danes?'

He had promised Hrothgar that he would not sleep until he had found Grendel's Mother and rid hall Heorot of the threat of Her.

Wealhtheow's last words had been: 'Take care. She was the wife of Cain. She is ten times more terrible than Her son.'

It was the smell of the fen, once he was out in it, that surprised Beowulf most. There were dry bones every-where amongst the marsh grasses, and the pools stank of centuries of decay. Yet this was not sufficient to account for the stench hanging over the miles and miles of desolation. It seemed to break from scummy bubbles lanced by the sun, and drift downwind, getting thicker. It made Beowulf cough. His horse shook its head. The golden bridle jingled.

At last the spoor came to an end.

Beowulf drew rein.

He stood beside a black rock that overhung the waters of a pool. The pool had dark veins of blood in it. There was a twisted tree on the rock. Dangling from the only branch that grew on the tree was a gory head. It was Unferth's. The eyes did not look sideways as they often had in life.

Beowulf spoke to his men.

'Bury Unferth's head,' he said. 'He was a person to be pitied.'

Some of the Geats wanted to argue, they hated the dead Dane so much. But when they saw their leader stripping off his blue cloak and obviously preparing to dive into the pool, they had no heart to question his commands.

Beowulf stared at the water. The blood was boiling in it, hissing like snakes. He guessed this must be Grendel's blood – the monster had plunged bleeding into the pool and drowned. And Unferth's head, as well as the spoor, told him that Grendel's Mother was down there too.

He rubbed at the ring on his finger. He said: 'Wait here for me for two days and two nights. If I do not come back to you before that time has passed, then I shall be dead and lost for ever and do not risk your lives in coming to look for me.'

His men promised that they would do as he said. None of them thought he would ever see Beowulf again. Their faces were strained and fearful – but Beowulf laughed before plunging headlong into the pool.

10
BEOWULF
AGAINST
GRENDEL'S
MOTHER

Down, down, down went Beowulf, deeper and deeper, and the water was getting darker and darker. He thought he would never come to the bottom. Perhaps there was no bottom, and he was falling into hell? Perhaps there was no way back? The water was foul, thick with blood and slime. The strange thing was that he could breathe the blood bubbles as they travelled past. They had a vile taste, but without them he would never have found sufficient breath to go so deep. He swam on. Soon he was far beyond any depth where the sun had ever shone. He shut his eyes because it was blacker with them open.

When Beowulf opened his eyes again there was a gleam of light below him. He kicked his way towards it. It grew, a ghostly green spot, bigger and bigger. Then it was all about him. It was alive, this light. It quivered. It throbbed.

It came off the wings of huge mothlike creatures drifting and looping in the underwater current. The creatures seemed blind. They did not attack him, but the cloud of them was so thick that he had to hack a passage through with his sword. Their wings flaked in the water, some stuck to him, some whirled about him, as he went on deeper into the pool.

She was waiting. She made no noise. Her tentacle arms were a part of the sucking, obsequious water.

Beowulf fell into them, as into a seaweed trap.

They closed about him tenderly. For a moment he succumbed, seduced by gentleness. Then, struggling to free himself, he found he could not. He kicked. Her grip tightened. She dragged him down.

Beowulf experienced a few seconds of sheer panic. There was no escaping, none, from these spongy intangible fingers that pulled him on, on, on, irresistibly insistent, coaxing, maternal. He could drown this way. She could choke him. She could squeeze the life from him. His face turned blue. Stars swam and spun in his brain . . .

Then he was gulping great lungfuls of air. Air! She had dragged him into Her den. The current loomed behind him, a liquid wall of black and green. Apparently, by some freak or witchcraft, it could not penetrate here. The cave went back a long way. Her arms stretched all along it, alive, like lichen.

Slowly She began to draw him down into the heart of the cave.

Beowulf snatched at his sword. Its jewels were sticky from Her vile embrace. It was difficult to hold. The hilt

54

slipped in his hand. Nevertheless, he managed to swing at the tentacles that gripped him. The blade bounced off. Her skin was too tough and scaly. He threw the sword away. It clattered against the wall. He could hear Her laughter, soft, malevolent, bloodthirsty.

He tried to get a grip on the rock floor, drag his heels, dig in with his toes, anything, but it was no good, no use; She kept on drawing him down into the dark, sucking at his skin, making kissing and swallowing noises, Her arms winding and unwinding about him like sinewy, swollen snakes.

Beowulf screamed with fright.

And the scream saved him. It brought him to his senses. It reminded him what he must do if he was not to be destroyed. He stopped shaking. He ceased his struggling. He let himself go dead in Her clammy grasp.

Grendel's Mother did not laugh now. She pulled him on more urgently. Some of his quiet strength communicated itself to Her terrible touch, and She sensed danger. But just what that danger was, and the doom it held in store for Her, She did not know until Beowulf began to speak, easily, boldly, in a voice that made the whole cave ring.

Beowulf said: 'I am Beowulf, son of Ecgtheow. I am Beowulf, the one sun-seeker. I am Beowulf, who killed Grendel. I did not fear the child of Cain. No more do I now fear You, who were once Cain's bride. No, nor would I fear the hideous Cain himself, if he had not been punished with lightning for the deed he did with You. Listen, She-evil, and I will tell You why this heart does not blush or blanch at the wicked worst You can do. It is because I, Beowulf, know myself. It is because I hold a

Cain in me, but do not let him out. That man is truly brave who, feeling fear, yet puts his fear to use and plucks new courage from the fear itself. That man is truly good who knows his own dark places.'

Grendel's Mother still dragged him down, but slower now, much slower. Her arms were losing power over him. She could feel Her magic going.

Beowulf said: 'There is a power You are powerless against. That power is in me. You see it shining in the golden collar about my neck. You feel it creeping through Your flesh, leaving You numb and cold. You think You hold me, She-evil, but in truth *I hold You!*'

So saying, he wound his square-tipped fingers firmly round one of the tentacles that gripped him. He felt the creature shudder as though suddenly touched by fire.

Her arms continued to draw him down, sluggishly.

He was nearing the deepest part of the cave.

He could make out the looming shape of Her.

He could see the eyes that glittered in Her breasts.

Beowulf stared into those terrible eyes. He did not blink or falter. His short sight helped him.

His strong hands tightened about the slimy tentacle.

Grendel's Mother sighed. A fetid breath of air passed through the chamber. Now that Beowulf was so close to Her the smell of sticky mother's milk was almost overwhelming. But he refused to be overwhelmed. He kept on tightening his grip. He kept on staring into the green corroding sea of Her eyes.

When he spoke again he put an equal emphasis on each word, so that it sounded like an incantation.

He said: 'I am Beowulf, son of Beowulf.'

The monster's eyes went cloudy.

He said: 'I am Beowulf, father of himself.'

The eyes were helpless. They flickered with sleep.

He said: 'I am Beowulf, who am myself.'

The eyes shut.

'Sleep,' said Beowulf softly. 'Sleep deep and never wake again.'

She slept.

Gently, carefully, with a stroking softness that was nearly pity, Beowulf puts his hands about Her neck, and strangled Her.

She did not fight. The tentacles went loose. They fell to the floor like useless ropes. Her body was melting. She was dead.

11
GRENDEL'S
HEAD

Beowulf stood back and wiped his hands on his golden collar. It was good to touch something good again. The collar absorbed the rusty stains of the monster's skin, and shone brighter than ever before.

Beowulf leaned his back to the wall. He was exhausted. His breath came deep. His heart was pounding. But he had never been so glad to hear it beating.

Gradually his eyes began to see into the thick dark that lay beyond the pool of what had once been Grendel's Mother. There was treasure there, but he did not want it. Only a huge sword caught his interest. It hung from a knob of rock. It was currved and terrible, far too heavy for mortal fighting, plainly the work of giants. He took it down with both hands, rested it between his knees, and ran his finger along its biting edge.

The sword made a sound like singing.

Deep in the underwater hall he heard another noise. A voice, as if in answer to the sword. A voice, but not forming words or syllables or any other kind of intelligible sound. It was a voice that spoke as ice speaks when it breaks on a winter tarn, or as men's bones speak when a killer cracks them. It was Grendel!

But Grendel was dead . . .

Grendel *was* dead, and it was his lifeless corpse, one arm torn out, that reared up quick in answer to the song of the sword, and sprang at Beowulf now!

Beowulf did not hesitate.

He lifted the giant sword in two hands and swung it. The sword flashed. Beowulf slashed. Grendel's dead head was severed from the shoulders of his dead body. Black blood gushed out and melted the giant blade as though it were no more than an icicle. Beowulf was left with only the hilt in his hand.

The corpse toppled over. It fell in the slime where only Her eyes were left.

Beowulf snatched up Grendel's head, stamped on Her eyes, and hurried from the cave.

High above, the red and black waters boiled and bubbled. Rain poured from a surly sky. Beowulf's men ringed the pool disconsolately. Their horses neighed and fretted to be gone.

One Geat said: 'No one could live in that. It's scalding hot.'

'So much blood,' said another. 'The She-monster has torn our lord in pieces.'

They could not look at each other.

'He must be dead.'

'Dead.'

'Yes. He must be dead.'

Just then, with a loud shout, Beowulf burst through the fiery scum at the pool's top.

He held Grendel's head up high.

His men were too astonished to raise a cheer. Some fell on their knees and offered thanks to God. But they cheered enough when they had helped the weary Beowulf from the water. The fen rang with their shouts of joy. The rain stopped. The sun came out. The waters of the lake subsided. Even the horses were inspired with the general happiness. They came round and poked at the monster's head with their muzzles. None was more curious than Beowulf's own mount, the white mare with the black mane.

It took four men to bear Grendel's head down to Heorot. They stuck their long spears in from different angles and carried it between them. Beowulf rode directly behind. Everyone sang.

Hrothgar and Queen Wealhtheow saw the happy triumphal procession afar off, and came galloping to greet it on sun-coloured horses. They both wept for joy when Beowulf told them all that had happened.

'Aeschere is avenged,' said Hrothgar. 'Heorot is saved.'

Wealhtheow, her blue eyes thoughtful, asked Beowulf what he had done with Unferth's head.

'Lady, it was buried,' Beowulf said.

The queen touched his hand where her ring still blazed on his finger. 'Beowulf,' she said, 'you are worthy of your great adventure.'

The king agreed wholeheartedly. He stretched out his arm and pointed to Heorot, its golden roofs intact and sparkling in the sun. 'Every man that lives or will live in time to come in this land of Danes will honour and praise your name, O Beowulf. Thank you, thank you, from the bottom of my heart.'

Queen Wealhtheow thanked Beowulf too. She noticed that his answering smile was a little twisted, as if with pain. 'Are you wounded?' she asked him, all concern.

Beowulf's grin broadened. 'Not by the monsters,' he replied.

'By what, then?' demanded Hrothgar, anxious to give the hero the best attention that it was in his power to give.

'By myself,' said Beowulf.

'Wounded by yourself?'

'By my own bad,' said Beowulf. He threw back his head and laughed in the sun, then winced. 'Please don't think of me as some sort of saint. That would make me as monstrous as Grendel, although in the other direction. Majesty of all the Danes, sweet Wealhtheow, you see before you a hero who has come through many kinds of high adventures only to fall foul of his own weakness.' He opened his mouth and poked one square-tipped finger in. 'All this excitement has given me a toothache!'

12
BEOWULF
GOES HOME

Next morning, Beowulf was woken by a hoarse sound, repeated over and over. It was like something grim and cheerless that has suddenly found within it a will to sing. He looked out of the window and saw a raven, black as soot, perched in the branches of a tree. The raven's breast was swollen with musical ambition, and its eyes were like little sparks. It flapped its wings vigorously and hopped up and down on a withered bough. Every now and again it managed an untuneful note.

Beowulf smiled, and gazed to the east where dawn was in the wind. 'Sing on, raven,' he said. 'Welcome morning as you can. You sound like my toothache, but welcome's no worse for that.'

Strange to tell, the raven now managed three ascending notes of great purity. Then it shook its wings as though casting off night for ever, took a couple of awkward steps, and flew away. At once, all the other birds began to sing. Beowulf touched his jaw in wonder. His toothache was gone.

Long light spilled across the fen. Beowulf considered it with a lump in his throat. This was not his country. He wanted to go home.

He went to Hrothgar and told him so.

Hrothgar was sad. He said: 'Beowulf, I love you as my own son. Why not stay here for ever, where your fame is?'

But Queen Wealhtheow did not seek to make him change his mind in this fashion. 'Beowulf's fame is wherever Beowulf is,' she said. 'Go home, hero, with our thanks and blessings.'

Then the king saw by the tears in Beowulf's eyes at the mere mention of the word 'home' that he did indeed pine for his own country. So he took Beowulf's hands between his own and blessed and thanked him as the queen had, his voice trembling with sincerity, and gave him twelve jewels – burning stones, the most precious things he owned.

'May your voyage be attended by white birds,' he said, tears trickling down his cheeks.

Beowulf was deeply moved. He saluted them both. 'Thank you,' he said. 'I shall not mind if the birds are black.' And he thought again of the raven that had tried to sing the dawn in.

The coastguard came to meet the marching men. 'God bless you, Beowulf,' he said simply. 'I am glad you did not take my advice and go home in the first place.'

Beowulf laid his hand on the coastguard's shoulder.

'Your advice was well meant,' he said, 'and I like your simplicity.' He looked eagerly at the bay. 'Is my ship prepared?'

'It is,' said the coastguard.

Room had to be made for the treasures Hrothgar had heaped on Beowulf, chiefly gold and horses. The coastguard helped with this. He was a huge man, with patient hands, and the horses trusted him even when their hooves were nervous of the tilting deck.

When all was ready Beowulf called the coastguard to him. 'On a little hill to the west,' he said, 'within sight of hall Heorot, you will find my sword. It is a good sword. Guard it well and it will guard you. I want you to have it.'

The coastguard thanked him. 'One question,' he said. 'Why did you go against Grendel without your sword?'

Beowulf smiled. 'On your advice, my friend.'

'My advice?' The coastguard frowned.

Beowulf dipped his hands in the sea. He let the cold green water drip through his cupped palms. 'It was you who told me that fighting Grendel was like fighting the sea itself,' he said. 'Well, then, who ever took a sword to kill the ocean?'

The sails opened. The tall mast rang. The great curved prow cut clean and quick through scudding foam. In such a vessel, coming back so happy from such a venture, they soon reached home.

When they did, Beowulf knelt on the beach and gathered up shingle in his fists and kissed it. Then he stood up and let his feet sink deep into soft sand. Then he ran along the shore, kicking shells in all directions. At last he came back to his men, panting, his face flushed, still grinning, not in the least ashamed of his boyish behaviour.

'It's good to be back home,' he said.

And they all agreed, and cheered.

They dragged down the wide sails. They set about the ship's unpacking.

The horses shivered on the new shore.

The gold was soon heaped so high, a man might not see over it to where the sun slipped into a sea flecked with black and white birds, the gulls that had followed them home.

13
KING
BEOWULF

King Hygelac's heart grew big with pride when he heard what Beowulf had done. Beowulf had always been his favourite nephew, even when he was a weak and sickly youth and no one else had any time for him. In those days the wits at Hygelac's court used to laugh at Beowulf: 'A silly boy! Fancy getting himself stung by bees! And always mooning about, dreaming of adventures, when he's not tall enough to win a tussle with a goat . . . He'll come to no good, you mark my words.' Beowulf *had* come to some good now, and those same court-wits had to eat their words when everyone learned what he had done against the monsters in the land of the Danes. King Hygelac ordered the most splendid feast his country had ever seen – and all in honour of brave Beowulf.

Beowulf was not greedy or ambitious. The gifts that Hrothgar had given him, he passed on to Hygelac. 'You are my king,' he said, 'and I am your man. All that I won, I won as your retainer. Here are horses, here is more gold than a man can carry. It is all for you, dear uncle.' He hesitated. Then he unbuckled the golden collar from about his neck – the Brisingamen collar that Queen Wealhtheow had given him. He held it up in the torchlight; it shone like a star-cluster. 'And this,' said Beowulf, 'I would give to you, dear aunt.'

Beowulf's aunt, Hygelac's young wife, was Hygd, the daughter of Haereth. Queen Hygd was beautiful and wise, with a creamy brow and poppies in her cheeks. She took the collar gladly, and thanked him for it.

Hygelac was so pleased and impressed by his nephew's courtesy that he granted to him as much land as he could cover in a day's ride on the white horse with the black mane. The mare flew over stone and stream and meadow, and by that sundown Beowulf was master of a greater estate in the land of the Geats than anyone save the king himself.

The only gift that Beowulf kept was the golden ring Queen Wealhtheow had put on his finger after the slaying of Grendel. He could not bring himself to part with this.

A few years passed in peace. Beowulf lived quietly, doing country things – he took to the keeping of bees, and most days would see him tending his tawny hives in the sun. The bees never stung him. They were big bees, too, armed with the kind of venom that could kill, if one was unfortunate enough to be attacked by the whole swarm. But Beowulf had a way with them, and the bees seemed to love him. Sometimes he would dust his cheeks with pollen and sprawl in the sun, and the bees used to come humming and crawl all over his face, so that anyone seeing him would swear he was wearing a mask of gold and black. He drank wine from a silver cup, never got drunk, and was very happy.

Then the peace was broken. The land of the Geats was invaded by the Friesians. The Friesians were fierce and cunning. They came in the night, their long ships creeping up the moonlit fjords. They burned and they plundered. They left death everywhere they went. But they always packed back to their ships and sailed away before Hygelac or Beowulf could catch them.

The king grew angry at these tricks. He led his men in a counter-attack. He burned whole villages in Friesland for revenge. But returning to his ship, he was trapped in an ambush. Hygelac fought desperately, for life was dear to him. But the Geats were outnumbered. Hygelac was killed. Beowulf himself just managed to escape, bearing his uncle's body, when all seemed lost. He had to swim back home through a half-frozen sea.

Queen Hygd was made sick with sadness at the loss of her husband. She was also worried because their only son, Hardred, was still a baby, unable to take more than a few faltering steps and say things like 'Mamma! Mercy, pity, peace, mercy, pity, peace ... Mamma!' and she saw a bloody fight coming, to determine who should rule the land. So she asked the people to set aside her own son's claim to the throne and have Beowulf as king.

The Geats cheered loud and long when they heard this. But Beowulf said: 'No, I am no usurper. I do not want the crown while anyone lives who has a better right to wear it.'

'Your feelings do you credit,' said Queen Hygd. 'But,

tell me, how can my son be king when he can hardly talk? How will he rule? Who will listen to him?'

Beowulf knelt by the boy Hardred, who was playing with some blocks upon the floor. 'I will listen to him,' he said seriously.

The baby looked at him.

Beowulf handed him a block.

'Mercy,' said Hardred.

'A fit quality in a king,' said Beowulf.

He handed the boy another block.

'Pity,' said Hardred.

'A wise virtue in a king,' said Beowulf.

He handed him a third block.

'Peace,' said Hardred.

'The end and purpose of all kingcraft,' said Beowulf.

He clapped his hands. Hardred laughed for joy and dropped the blocks. Beowulf lifted him in his arms and set him on his shield. Then he raised both, shield and baby, above his head.

'Long live Hardred!' he cried. 'Long live any monarch who learns to speak of mercy, pity, and peace while still in his mother's arms. People, behold your king! Beowulf will uphold and protect him as long as he lives!'

Hardred grew up to rule as a good king should. He was kind and firm and generous, brave in battle, gentle in the company of women, straight in his every dealing. Anyone was always welcome at his court. This, unfortunately, proved his undoing, for one day he was visited by the sons of Othere, the man who discovered the North Cape. They had quarrelled with their father, and rebelled against their uncle Onela, king of Sweden. They wanted asylum.

Hardred took pity on the two young men, doomed to wander the face of the earth because of a family feud. He said they could stay at his court for as long as they wished. Their names were Eanmund and Eadgils, and they showed themselves genuinely grateful to Hardred for this hospitality.

But when King Onela heard that his rebellious nephews had obtained sanctuary in Hardred's land, he flew into a rage. He tore at his beard and rolled on the ground in his fury. Then he took ship at the head of a band of fighting men, and set sail for the kingdom of the Geats.

Hardred was killed by Onela's axe in the bitter battle that followed. Eanmund was kiled too, and Eadgils fled away. But King Onela was reluctant to meet Beowulf face to face in mortal combat, and anyway he had achieved what he had set out to do, so he withdrew while things were still going well for him.

After the battle, before the smoke had died from Hardred's funeral pyre, the Geats sent again to Beowulf, asking him if he would be king. This time he said yes.

14
THE
FIREDRAKE

Beowulf wanted peace. He liked the days he could spend with his bees, and the summer sun, and the way night came gentle from the dusky sea. He had seen enough of wars and quarrels and sudden death. He longed for quiet – to be able to stand by a blue pool in the evening, and lob a pebble into the water, and watch the circles of ripples spread slow on the sober surface. Yet he regretted Hardred's killing. His conscience would not let him rest till he had avenged that. So he sent word to Eadgils in exile, and helped him with men and equipment, and plotted a campaign for him. The fighting was fierce and long, but in the end Eadgils won. He killed Onela in fair combat. At last all the kingdoms of the north could live in friendship.

Beowulf enjoyed the peace he wanted. For forty years the land was happy and undisturbed. A generation of children grew up who knew no more of violence than picking flowers and tumbling on the sands. Wives were concerned with the snowy produce of the washing tub. Old soldiers – some of them survivors of that brave fourteen who had gone with Beowulf against Grendel – sat with their ale in the evening under golden-budded oaks and fought over battles long ago. It was a good age to live in, everyone agreed.

Beowulf was now an old man. His beard was white. His back was bent. He was nearly blind. He had done nothing much for forty years but tend his bees. The bees had taught him, he said, to rule wisely. There was order and beauty in the world of bees. He had tried to bring some of that to the world of men.

But there was one person in the land of the Geats who was not happy. He was a slave, and he had been threatened with a beating for doing something wrong. He did not like being beaten, so he ran away. He climbed high into the mountains to hide.

Now, nobody usually ventured into the mountains because long ago one of them had been opened up and used as a burying place for princes. As was the custom, all their treasures had been buried with them – gold and silver swords and jewelled cups. People believed that it was best to leave such places alone. The treasure had been given back to the earth, and it would be a sin to steal it.

The slave was desperate. He did not care about any of this. He clambered up over storm-lashed rocks. The place was wild. Huge blocks of stone lay everywhere, piled against the mountainside, threatening to fall, strewn about as though hurled by giants in some dreadful battle. At last he got to the top. This was where the treasure had been buried.

He crept inside a narrow crack in the rock. It was like being inside a demon's mouth. Teeth tore at him as he wriggled along. They may have been no more than sharp ridges in the walls of the passage, but to the slave, alone and frightened in the dark, they seemed alive and snapping. Something did not welcome his presence here. His scalp prickled. His spine felt like an icicle. But there was no going back.

He came into a natural chamber. The light dazzled his eyes. The chamber was crammed with treasure. On the floor, in the middle of a maze of gold, sat a lizard.

The slave felt panic flooding through his limbs as the lizard's eyes swivelled to look at him. He grabbed the nearest thing to hand – a jewelled cup big enough to bathe a baby in – and turned, and squeezed into the flaw in the rock.

There was a fury at his heels. The lizard hissed and swelled. Fire poured from its mouth. It was not a lizard at all. It was the Firedrake, most evil of creatures that haunt the burying places of men!

The slave's hair caught fire in the blast of flame the Firedrake sent to follow him. He screamed. But he clung on tight to the cup. He had one thought – if he took this prize back to his master, he might escape the whipping. It must be worth a lot.

He struggled out into open air and plunged his head straight into a mountain stream. Then he set off as fast as he could, scrambling down the rocks, the cup clutched to his chest.

The mountain shook with the raging of the Firedrake. Its scaly body swelled and swelled as it got angrier. It had gold eyes and a thrashing tail. Flames came teeming from its mouth, and molten spit, and reeking, scorching smoke. The effect was like a volcano.

Fortunately for the slave, the creature's swollen state prevented the Firedrake from following him through the fissure in the rock. If this had not been so, the thief would have been roasted alive.

15
BEOWULF AGAINST THE FIREDRAKE

By nightfall the Firedrake managed to cool its temper. It crawled out from its den and stood on top of the mountain. Its gold eyes flared like meteors in the dusk. It was a long time since it had needed to leave the glittering hoard it gloated over. Deep in its tiny brain a coal of evil began to glow. It wanted revenge. It looked down at the lights in the valley, the houses of the peaceful country-folk. They seemed to form the shape of a great jewelled cup. The creature lashed its tail in fury. It spread its wings, and swooped.

Houses, churches, fields of grain, nothing was spared by the Firedrake in its ruinous flight. People woke up to find fire at their windows, and ran from their doors howling warning, only to encounter the same flames everywhere, leaping and lapping, laying the countryside bare. In the morning, when the Firedrake flapped back to its den, the valley looked like a basin of white ashes. Even the streams had caught fire and burned away.

They brought the slave to Beowulf, and he told his story. When he had finished, and his master had shown the king the stolen cup, some of the lords of the court cried out that the slave should be offered to the Firedrake as a sacrifice.

Beowulf hummed, then said: 'No, let him eat honey.'

Most of those present looked curiously at the king, and muttered among themselves, thinking him mad. 'He is too old,' said one. 'His wits are warped.'

Only Wiglaf, son of Weohstan, had a good word for Beowulf. 'By saying the slave should eat honey,' he explained, 'he means that we should find a little pity in our hearts for one who was driven by despair to do something he will always regret.'

'All the honey in the world can't sweeten the bitterness this wretch has brought down upon us,' said one of the old soldiers. 'It means the old days are back. War and strife and pestilence, that's what it means. You're young, Wiglaf, and you don't know what you're talking about.'

Wiglaf flushed. 'It's true I've had no experience of battle,' he said, 'but I'm sure I'd prove as brave as you.'

'Well,' sneered the soldier, 'no one ever won a wound by boasting, eh? Young Wiglaf against the Firedrake! That should be a fight worth watching! When are you going to volunteer?'

Wiglaf bit his lip.

Beowulf silenced them all with a wave of his hand. He might be an old man, but he still carried authority. 'I will go against the Firedrake,' he said.

Nobody dared to argue.

Beowulf began buckling on his armour. His huge hands shook. Wiglaf had to help him. The young man could not help remarking that Beowulf's body had shrunken with age. His coat of mail hung loose from his stooping shoulders. But his heart, thought Wiglaf, was as big and brave as it had always been – that would never shrink.

Beowulf said nothing. He hummed to himself. He was thinking of a tale he had heard long ago, in Hrothgar's court, at the time of the celebrations occasioned by his victory over Grendel: the tale of Sigemund and little Fitela, and how they had outwitted the Fire Dragon. Patiently he began to form a plan in his mind.

The old warriors murmured together. For all their complaining, they loved Beowulf, and they could not bear the thought of his going alone to what looked like certain death.

A spokesman stepped forward. 'Twelve of us,' he said, 'want to come with you.'

Beowulf nodded absentmindedly. 'Good, good.'

'If swords are any use, then –'

'They aren't,' said Beowulf.

'Oh.' The soldier was flabbergasted.

'But you can carry the hives,' said Beowulf.

'The – *hives?*'

'That's right.'

Beowulf stood up. 'Wiglaf,' he said.

'My lord?'

'You come too.'

They climbed up into the mountains. Beowulf went slowly, leaning on Wiglaf's shoulder. The other twelve followed behind, each man struggling with one of the enormous hives on his back. Wiglaf, on Beowulf's instructions, carried a newly cut stake, about six feet long, and a glove that would have fitted a giant. None of the others knew what these were for, and they all thought privately that Beowulf had gone quite mad in having them venture, thus equipped, against a monster that could breathe fire. Beowulf said nothing by way of explanation. He chuckled as he told Wiglaf the story of Sigemund and Fitela. He said: 'They used their wits, you see. If you can't beat evil by strength alone, then a little cunning is called for.'

Wiglaf told his king how black the burnt-out valley looked below. Beowulf nodded sadly. 'No one can bring back the living who were lost,' he said, 'yet some good can be plucked from the worst disaster. The Firedrake will pay for what it has done – not only with its life, but with the gold it keeps watch over. What good does gold do, buried in the earth? When we have killed the creature, we will use that treasure to build again each dwelling that is gone.'

An eagle drifted high overhead. Young Wiglaf looked from the eagle to his master, and back again. Beowulf was bent and breathless. The eagle was king of the air. Yet, thought Wiglaf, there was not so much difference between them.

16
BEES

Beowulf halted his men when they came to the crack that led to the Firedrake's den. He had them set the hives down in the entrance. Then he sat for a while, muttering to the bees in each hive. No one could make out what he said. It sounded like nonsense.

At last, just as the stinking sun came level with the crags behind them, he motioned for Wiglaf to go forward.

The lad, acquainted with his master's plan, slipped into the crack. He carried the white stake in his left hand. In his right hand, and very carefully, as though it contained something infinitely precious, he carried the giant glove.

The others were too puzzled to protest. They noticed that the bees in each hive buzzed busily as Wiglaf wriggled past them. Beowulf stooped and murmured soothingly and the noise subsided.

Once inside the narrow passageway, Wiglaf moved on

tiptoe, deftly. He was a small person, slim and agile, which was partly why Beowulf had chosen him for the job. When he came to the bright treasure-chamber he skipped into it like a shadow. As it happened, the Firedrake was asleep – worn out by its night's havoc – and did not see him hide himself amid the gold.

Beowulf was watching the sun. When he judged that enough time had elapsed for Wiglaf to have performed the first part of the plan successfully, he crept into the crack himself. He set his horn to his lips and blew a loud, rude blast.

'Haloo,' he cried. 'Haloo, old fire-belcher! I am Beowulf, come to quench you!'

The Firedrake's golden eyes snapped open. It could not believe that anyone would be so foolhardy as to shout at it inside the mountain.

Beowulf sounded another mocking note on his horn. 'Ho, you, old smoky-guts! Where are you hiding?'

The Firedrake hissed with rage. No one had ever spoken to it like this before. Its tail began to flog the rock. Its body started to swell in the usual way.

Peeping from his hiding place, little Wiglaf waited anxiously for the right moment. He could hear the grumbling fire beginning in the creature's belly. Smoke was whistling from its nostrils. It was getting bigger every moment. Wiglaf crouched, ready to pounce.

'Call yourself a dragon?' shouted Beowulf. 'You look more like a glow-worm!'

The Firedrake had reached full size. When it heard this final insult, it swallowed hard in its fury.

Wiglaf seized his chance. He leapt.

Quick as lightning he thrust the big stake in the

Firedrake's jaws, jamming them open even as the creature gaped wide to let loose the first foul gust of flame. The golden eyes glared at this new surprise. The barbed tail thrashed and twisted to be at him. But Wiglaf dodged, danced, flitted out of range. And as he went he threw the giant glove into the open mouth.

The Firedrake coughed. A hail of cinders flew out. For a terrible moment Wiglaf thought the glove had come out too – but, no, it was still there, caught on a tooth that looked like a scythe.

As Wiglaf watched, the glove flapped and bulged.

Beowulf made a high-pitched buzzing sound.

The Firedrake took a deep breath . . .

. . . and swallowed a big Queen Bee that emerged from the glove as if in answer to Beowulf's call!

'They follow the Queen Bee *anywhere!*' This, whispered to Wiglaf on the way up the mountain, was the essence of Beowulf's plan. Now, in response to another noise he made, sawing at his lips with his square-tipped fingers, all the twelve hives came alive. The bees poured out, a singing angry stream, orange, brown, black, yellow. They buzzed into the crack in the mountain.

They whirled past Beowulf. And on into the brightness of the treasure-chamber.

The Firedrake saw them coming. Its gold eyes bulged with fright. It tried to shut its mouth, but the stake between its jaws prevented this.

The bees poured down the monster's throat like a stream of honey, in pursuit of their queen. But when they reached the Firedrake's stomach their effect was like no honey in the world.

81

They began to sting!

Hundreds of bees, stinging it from the inside!

The Firedrake roared with pain and fury.

It tried to spit out bees. But there were too many.

It tried to spew up fire. But its own insides were burning.

Little Wiglaf danced with glee.

But Beowulf had collapsed in the entrance to the treasure-chamber. His armour came undone. It was all too big and heavy for him.

Some men said, long afterwards, that Beowulf was killed by the burning breath of the Firedrake. But, in truth, the monster managed only the merest tiny little cough of smoke before turning over on its side and giving up the ghost. Beowulf's bees had stung it to death.

Wiglaf knelt by his master's side.

Beowulf chuckled. 'A pretty trick,' he said. 'Listen, Wiglaf. When I was young I'd never have done a thing like that. I'd have thought it was dishonourable, or something. Well, the dragon lies dead, and the treasure is there for the good of our people. Who was right? Old Beowulf, or young Beowulf?'

Wiglaf said: 'Both.'

Beowulf was quiet for a while. His eyes seemed to overflow with the dazzling light off the treasure, and tears ran down his cheeks.

'A pity about the bees,' he said at last. 'I loved them.'

'They died well, master,' Wiglaf said. Then he began to laugh. He could not help or stop himself. 'What a trick!' he cried. 'Who ever would have thought of it!'

Beowulf winked one watery eye. 'Perhaps it's better

82

that nobody should just now,' he said. 'Tell them what you like, the ones out there, but remember the world will need to be a little older before it understands this last exploit of Beowulf. Yes, and all the others too! Meanwhile, it must have an ordinary kind of hero to believe in. Make sure you give them that, Wiglaf. It will serve for now. And one day – who knows how far ahead? – if my name should live, someone will stumble on this story and put the pieces together again, and come up with the truth of it.'

Wiglaf shook his head. 'I doubt it,' he said. 'Not this last bit, anyway.'

'Beowulf,' said Beowulf. 'Beowulf, the bee-hunter. Well, it might occur to somebody.'

The buried Beowulf's body in a great green fist of land that struck out into the sea. And they heaped white stones upon it, to show how much they had loved him. In the years that followed, the place became a well-known landmark for mariners. Men would point to it on the way to sea, saying: 'There is Beowulf's grave.' And no one saw it without feeling an inch taller where he stood.

Wiglaf never told the whole story about the bees. He became king in Beowulf's stead, and ruled wisely and well to the end of his days. When people asked him this or that about the dead hero, he had one way of answering – with a little puzzling smile in his eyes as he silently recalled a golden stream of bees disappearing down a dragon's throat. 'Beowulf,' he said, 'was Beowulf.'

'Come now,' the more curious people protested,

smelling a mystery. 'There must have been more to it that that.'

'No more, no less,' said Wiglaf. 'Beowulf was Beowulf.' And that was all he would say, ever.

Note

Beowulf is the longest surviving poem in Old English, an epic recording the great deeds of its warrior hero. It was first written down round about 1000 A.D. in the West Saxon dialect, but might have existed in oral form for centuries before that.

There are many literal versions of the story in modern English. I have not tried to compete with them. This is an interpretation, not a translation.

Myth seems to me to have a peculiar importance for children, as for poets: it lives in them. I have tried to have this telling for children as a living thing. In sticking to the text of the original epic, it may be loose. In sticking to the root-meaning of that poem, I trust that it is tight.

One retells mythic stories hoping to be rewarded with the discovery that their meaning is still alive. I feel that in writing this version I discovered something about *Beowulf* which might be said to be new as well as old. I hope that you, reader, will find what I found and make it your own. Remember, stories like this belong to all of us, so are never to be told in final form.

R.N.